CW01336547

Copyright © 2021 Flora Cruft

The moral right of Flora Cruft to be identified as the author of this work has been asserted in accordance with the Copyrights, Designs and Patents Act of 1988.

All rights reserved. No part of this publication may be reproduced, stored in a retrieval system, or transmitted in any form or by any means, electronic, mechanical, photocopying, recording, or otherwise, without the prior permission of the both the copyright owner and the above publisher of this book.

First published in Great Britain in 2021 by amato & muldown
amatoandmuldown.com | amatoandmuldown@gmail.com

An imprint of The Mum Poem Press
themumpoempress.com | themumpoempress@gmail.com

A CIP catalogue record for this book is available from the British Library.

ISBN 978-1-8382888-5-3

amato & muldown is an independent publisher of collections by individual poets. Established in 2021 by the founders of the Mum Poem Press and the6ress, we offer poets expertise in building, publishing and marketing their collections.

FLORA CRUFT

I am a Spider Mother

amato & muldown

"Every mother contains her daughter in herself, and every daughter her mother, and every mother extends backwards into her mother, and forwards into her daughter."

Carl Jung

"My best friend was my mother and she was deliberate, clever, patient, soothing, reasonable, dainty, subtle, indispensable, neat and as useful as a spider."

Louise Bourgeois

For my mother and my daughters

Flora Cruft is a poet whose work has been published in a variety of anthologies, magazines and journals. She has performed her poetry at venues such as Shakespeare & Co, Paris; The Poetry Café, London; and Exeter Phoenix in Devon.

Flora is also an existential psychotherapist and a creativity coach in private practice. She has an Instagram page @poet.therapist.baker where she explores the intersections between poetry, mental health, maternity, creativity and nutritional psychology. A mother to twins, she lives in East Devon with her partner and family.

Nomi McLeod is an illustrative artist who works mainly through drawing. Her work attempts to give visual form to both hidden, inner worlds and collective stories of the external world. She lives in Devon with her partner, their daughter and twin sons.

Contents

    Two Lockets   15

Spiderling:

Happiness	21
Hurricanes Can Be Heard Under Water	23
Easter Bathers	24
Into the Garden	25
Initiation	27
Ballad of the Dinner Table	29
What Type of Woman are You?	30
Journey	33

Spider:

A Catch	39
In Vitro	40
Cardiotocography	42
Full Moon	44
The Prophecy	45
It's 4am	46
Velvet Spider	48
The New Twin Mum: an incomplete glossary	50
The First Lesson	51

Web:

My mother's dressing gown	57
Dress Up	59
Portrait of My Parents as House Plants	60
From the Mouths of Babes	61
It ends here	62
Sister Sister	63
Grandmothergram	64
Maman	65
Night Birds	66

Two Lockets
After Ted Hughes

Inside the new locket, the twin girls.
Inside the twin girls, the open smiles.
Inside the open smiles, the gaps of gum.
Inside the gaps of gum, the throats of silk.
Inside the throats of silk, the budding voices.
Inside the budding voices, the branches of blood.
Inside the branches of blood, the pulsing hearts.
Inside the pulsing hearts, my bitten lips.
Inside my bitten lips, the cribellate web.
Inside the cribellate web, the years spun waiting.
Inside the years spun waiting, the strength rising.
Inside the strength rising, my grandmother's locket.
Inside my grandmother's locket, my mother's arms.
Inside my mother's arms, my babyhood.
Inside my babyhood, my throat of silk.
Inside my throat of silk, my budding voice.
Inside my budding voice, my branches of blood.
Inside my branches of blood, my heart's pulse.
Inside my heart's pulse, my mother being born.

Spiderling

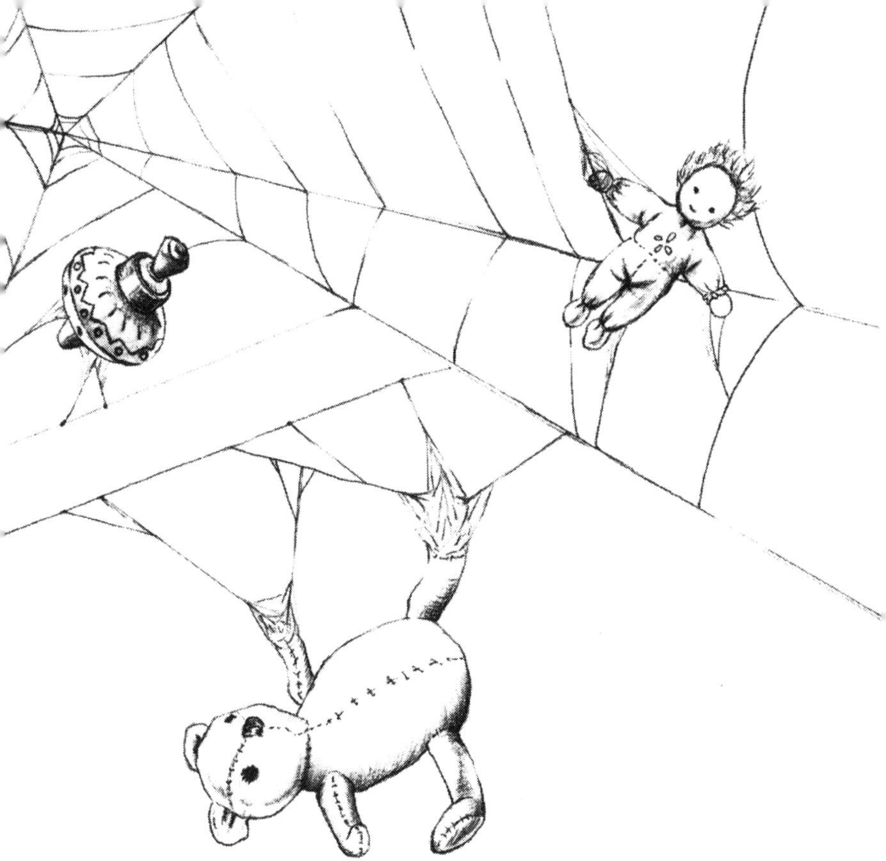

Happiness

That green, green caravan.
Chipped paint and the smell
of burning sausages.
A carpet of wild grasses and flowers
spread before me,
how I love this place.
The horses in the adjoining field
watch in bemusement
as I place my spindly seven year old foot
onto Titania's carpet
and throw myself into the air
the fauvist ballerina, arched
hands and pirouetting limbs,
flying through the sky
rolling in the earth,
grasping fistfuls of grass, readying myself
to consume the world.
In my ears, my eyes, my mouth
I taste its mellow honey.
My mother claps her hands in smiles,
beautiful tanned icon
in cheesecloth red.
Perhaps one day, if I laugh enough,
I will be that woman.

Now all is preparation.
I am singing as I dance,
I embrace the air
and it plays with me,
my dark curls blowing high above my head,
a tall crown. Queen of the flowers – Flora!
My brothers join in, moving their bodies
like mad little warriors
fighting an unseen force.
The bonfire my father built burns holes into the dusk.

Hurricanes Can Be Heard Underwater

Spiderfish swim on my wall
In the drowsy heat
I open a door.
damp and muted with sleep,
slipping her over me
The high pitch

plump as rosebuds
I rise from my body,
There are my parents in their bed
I step neatly into my mother,
like a dress.
air thickens to howl

When my father falls
there is a judder in him,
I watch his legs
a cliff face crumbling
His eyes find mine

for the first time
some inner machinery halts.
release
into the sea.
I catch his fear as he falls

Easter Bathers

They tug off their clothes, shedding all
except instinct, and rush into the sea.

Laughter runs before them, bubbling the air.
The sea's tongue licks the little bodies,

lifts them up on high foamed haunches
so that they seem not to touch the water

but float bare above. Luminous tangle
of emboldened flesh, strands of hair woven with seaweed.

Stumbling back out, one of them has cut her knee.
She sits by her mother, sewn up in a huddle of towels,

staring at the peeling skin and purplish depth
wondering whether to touch it.

Into the Garden

I've run away with myself,
I don't know where I'm going.
This rainbow rucksack holds
my crumpled Wonder Woman cape
and a magnifying glass, cracked in one corner.

I snuck out while Mum was making tea.
Mash and peas, ketchup
dolloped beneath the nose
of a grilled sausage –
my favourite.

She'll start calling us soon,
push her voice to reach every corner
of our ears. My big brother
practises his violin to the impatient tick
of a metronome;

the little one lines toy cars
in order of size at Mum's feet,
jeeps behind lorries in a traffic jam,
as a spider no bigger than his thumb
scuttles out from beneath the wheels.

Out in the breeze, libraries of flowers
line my path.
I read their faces
as I sway on my stalk.
The garden gate swings open.

Initiation

My abdomen screwed too tightly
to my legs, no way

to escape this pelvis; I must
lie on the bed, and bleed.

The house is full of boys.
My mother brings her hot water bottle,

the rubber scales slosh
on my belly, a fish roasted

whole from her sea spider's catch.
She hands me her tools:

pads to hold clots thick as algae,
tampons with tadpole tails.

An hour earlier
I'd have turned away from her,

cut myself
from her fastening web.

Now I'm the stuck fly,
crying for her to stop up a curse,

the first wave
of the threatening tide.

Ballad of the Dinner Table

I am only wood they expect so much from me /
place their hands / carve animals / spit upon me
I am only wood they bring themselves to me /
in conversation / in greed / they hold me
I am only wood they lay unclean / upon me /
unblock their voices / throw questions /
carve their needs into my flat / open / face
I am only wood I can be / stained / stoic / rowdy
I am only wood wiped by a woman's cloth /
draped / for celebration / for nourishment
I am only wood freckled with the detritus of life /
books / bills / homework / her hands take it all
I am only wood my mouth metal / the soldier knives /
straight fork tines / jump / to meet her touch
I am only wood I welcome / teenagers / leftovers /
the sway / as the family sets their feast / to toast /
the mother / they love / the fetus / she must abort /
the broken lamb / amongst the mint sauce

What Type of Woman are You?

1. As you catch sight of yourself in a Topshop changing room, which Disney character do you most resemble?

   a. Rapunzel in the tower
   b. Shrek
   c. Belle, pursued by Gaston and pitchforked villagers
   d. Snow White, tasting the apple
   e. All of the above
   f. None of the above

2. What would your super power be?

   a. People pleaser = acceptance junkie
   b. Rebel in search of a cause = multiple piercings
   c. Study hound = intimacy avoidant
   d. Happy go lucky = eat the feelings
   e. All of the above
   f. None of the above

3. What did your parents tell you about sex?

   a. Don't smile at strangers
   b. Wait until you're ready
   c. You'll have conflicting desires, opposable thumbs
   d. Single mums don't get degrees

e. All of the above
   f. None of the above

4. What's your favourite thing to do at night?

   a. Wank to a picture of Keanu Reeves
   b. Go clubbing with friends
   c. Look at your naked body by candlelight
   d. Squeeze blocked facial pores
   e. All of the above
   f. None of the above

5. What's your favourite sexual position?

   a. Holding hands
   b. Girl on top
   c. Tit grope on the tube
   d. Doggy style
   e. All of the above
   f. None of the above

6. Do you have hair on your:

   a. Legs
   b. Pudenda

c. Nipples

d. Neck

e. All of the above

f. None of the above

7. Who is your female icon?

a. Beyoncé

b. Nigella Lawson

c. Any witch, burnt at any stake

d. Louise Bourgeois's Maman sculpture

e. All of the above

f. None of the above

Journey

I push my way through
the blue hedgerows
and wild garlic,
down the potholed lanes
and low of cattle,
past mossy streams,
my footprints sealed
in the cloying mud,
my suitcase carried
over the station's curve
into the dark
womb of a train
to a land of a different dirt;
cherry laced Doc Martens
scuffed against club floors,
kick up my tireless bloom.

Spider

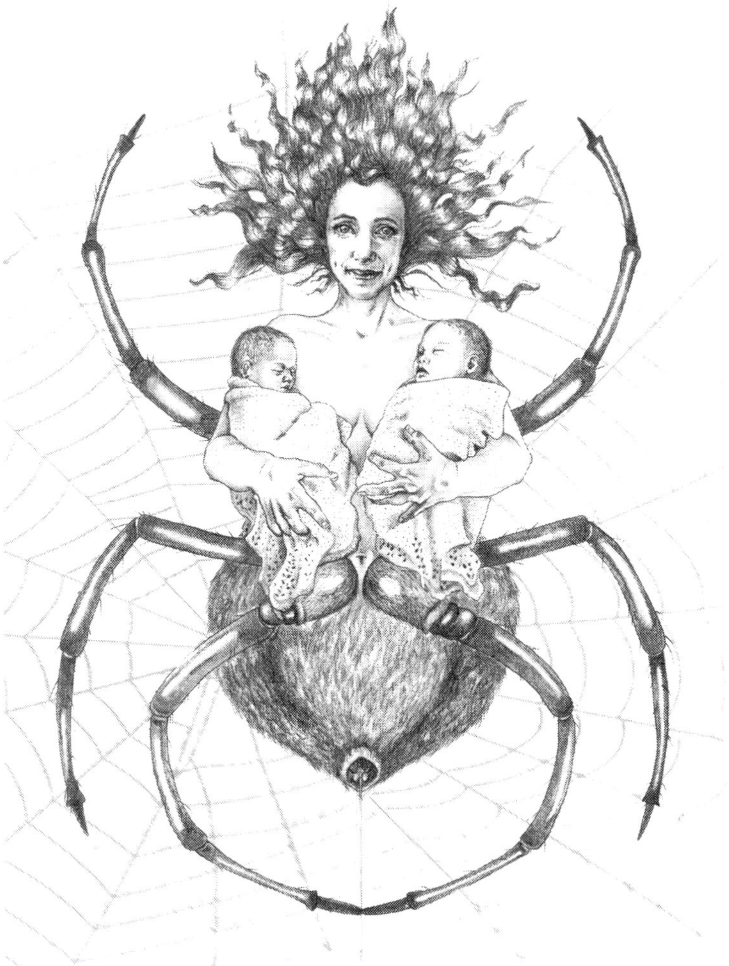

A Catch
For James

                You're the only one
                who never worried
                that I'd eat you.
                Not that you aren't
                delicious to me –
                golden muscle
                against my black
                fuzz. You come
                a willing feast,
                worth more alive.

In Vitro

The bones of life grow
out of such exquisite loss.
Doctors said there was nothing
wrong, nothing at all;
the bright light of nothing
shone through every scan,
ultrasound probe prodding
its brisk phallus against the walls
of my uterus
to sweep me clean.

There was nothing I could do
but wait, hope and
pay to be filled,
yet the babies would not rest,
they swam free from me
I felt them leave, as limbs that
move in slumber
break the night.

Each day I'd mix my potions,
lay out new needles
break fresh bruises on the veiny
maps of my thighs.
Stabbing through skin
I joined centuries of hopeful women,
felt their tears pool my eyes,
their words beneath my breath
What spell to use? Which way
to pick the lock at maternity's door?

Cardiotocography

The noise overwhelms me
                         vibrations of your ocean drum
each note
                         plays a different frequency, each note
ululates a ripple
                         only I discern.
This is how you speak to me,
                         through the beat
                         of your ripening heart
Dum-Da Dum-Da
                         Mum-Ma Mum-Ma.
Below my bloated pressure stockinged feet
                         sits a machine spewing out images:
a chain of dark mountains
                         rough tumbles from the peak
the shadow of an eagle
                         hung in empty air.
I hold tight to the hem of this blue
                         checked gown but it's no use,
my mind rushes
                         as you contract the muscle
                         of my blood.

You jump on my cord
                like a restless hare.
Behind us I hear the call
                        of another, racing to catch up.

Full Moon

We enter every space ahead of her, our round silhouette an announcement, followed by her swollen legs, milky way breasts, her cheeks flushed suns, quicksilver eyes held up in silent prayer to the cosmos, her hands the stars that orbit our globe like we're her only way home.

The Prophecy

May you have twins / the third magpie sang / and though it was a curse / it was a blessing / seven months in found me bloated / beached in the pre-eclamptic heat / then they opened me up / pulled out a frenzy / four spindle legs / four crooked arms / kicking / searching for sister / craving her smell / I caught a glimpse as I held your Daddy's hand / then down you went in heated boxes / wheeled away / while on the post op table I lay / salted and lanced / exorcised of fevers / your first cries ringing through the corridor / like moths bombing the flickering bulb of my mind / and I was myself again / so they said

It's 4am

I hold a newly made baby
like a grenade in my arms.
Another lies in her cot
crying for me.

Bubbles of tears coat her face,
she is a part of me I crave to reach.

Yet I am with her sister now
who feeds in great gasps,
accustoms herself sleepily
to a milk that is not mine.

The baby in her cot
is turning pink, fluorescent
in her loneliness. I send out
my voice to hold her

my words are fingers
they trace around her need

                let it exist
"I'm here"
                her feelings are fur balls stuck
                    in her throat

"It's ok"
               cravings
                             dance in her downy cheeks
"Mummy's coming"
               one big retch
                             and the suffering is out, vomited
                             into the room

I carefully place the fed baby down,
scuttle over to attach myself to her twin.

My limbs have grown long and strong
               I am a spider mother.

Velvet Spider

In the darkest corner she crouches, hairy
haunches tense and ready.
Hers are the legs of an athlete
black exoskeleton trained to hold the softness
in, her frame of bones a shield to keep out all
except offspring.

When spiderlings emerge, translucent
from their shedded skins, she taps the knotted web
to wake an urge in them, break them
from their womb-dreams
with a jolt. She must chant and sing
walk long limbs in circles,

lay out the fruit of her chest
to appease those tiny gods.
See how she presses herself against her babies
how they climb atop her skin,
burrow face down
to love the meat between her ribs.

They will eat their fill until the juice drains
from her legs, for she must reach her peak:
consummation. The memory of her own
mother in her mouth as
she is sucked and liquefied; little fangs
pierce with such sweet venom.

The New Twin Mum:
an incomplete glossary

Appetite: endless.
Breakfast: little mouths open like beaks for a worm.
Colic: the sound of cats mating.
Dummies: soothe me.
Evening: rock a bye.
Fury: the constant crying.
Ga Ga Goo Goo: dawn chorus.
Hatred: a friend's baby sleeps through the night.
Incredible: that they're still alive.
Joy: mother's heroin.
Kitchen: a bombsite.
Lunch: yesterday's mash and baked beans from the tin.
Memory: absent without leave.
Nipples: tingle at the sight of downy bodies.
Overwhelmed: by everything.
Premature: hooked up in hospital.
Quiet: never.
Rest: don't be silly.
Skin: velvet upon velvet upon kiss upon kiss.
Teething: my nightly wail and grind.
Umbilical cords: cut but not forgotten.
Vomit: all over the health visitor.
Wind: old man farts from miniature bottoms.
X: rated language at the Calpol bottle.
Yes: to all this, and much more.
Zzzzz: sleep a memory to hold close, as I hold my babies closer.

The First Lesson

When the instructor shouts
        and you jump into the pool
                without knowing how to swim,
                        what do you tell yourself?

Head down like a stone
        eyes surprised by acerbic chlorine,
                bee stings
                      against open nostrils.

In the lustre of the deep end
        I see you, a stout infantfish
                searching for your scales,
                      limbs kicking up toothless shadows.

What makes you rise
        to hold life's beauty for a float?
                There's strength in
                      your certainty, if not in your tiny toes.

You love the water as it tries to drown you.

Web

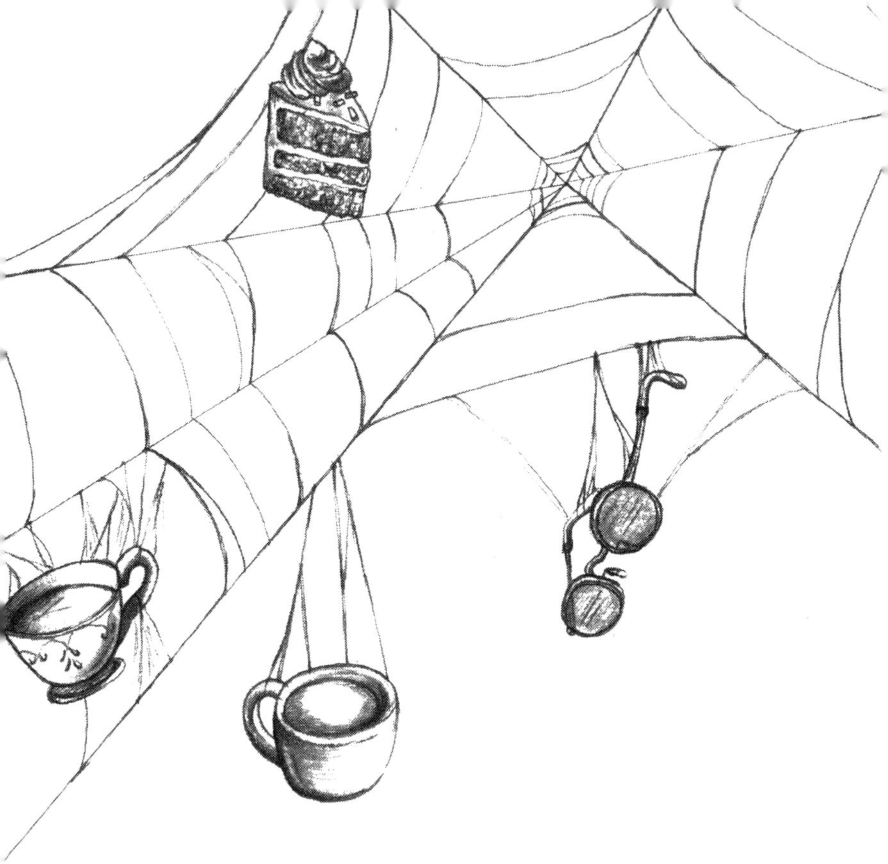

My mother's dressing gown

is soft, good to rub against.
Only one stain on the velveteen,
only two patches where the fabric wears thin.
Here she keeps her spider heart, stretched large
and flat through years of service
but still pumping,
still dazzling as a furnace
still kind as oxygen.

When my children rummage the pockets
they find plasters and Savlon,
hair brushes, enough
to fuel a family. They file their fingers
to sharpness with her nail file, magnify their pores
in her mirror to see her face shining back –
she is their other mother.

Wrapped in her gown, my mother grows new blooms
on her septuagenarian skin. Skin tags
and melanoma crusts, burnt
mementos of the sun, some cut off,
some she welcomes in.
I scan her body for visitors, fear
the one to break our web.

We are torch bearers at teatime,
holding our flames to the children's faces.
I learn to mother when I watch her throw fire –
the heat enough to singe my brows
the hot soil of her arms my place to be planted.

Dress Up

Sun through the glass
doorway, Ribena for wine
and your granddaughters giggling.

One hooks your pink M&S bra
over her school dress. It hangs on her
thin length, cupping nothing.

She wears your sunglasses, and the swing
of your hips as you walk down the street
in your best legs and bootcut jeans.

Her sister, swathed in shawl and the Radio Times,
makes a nest from cushions
and the wings of broken moths.

When you see them, your face breaks open.
You with your joy
and our girls playing wise.

Portrait of my Parents as House Plants

She is spider, lean and many-legged.
Her honeydew sap sticks to everyone.
                He is tall as a money plant
                should be, with heart shaped leaves
                like coins that sit in my hand.
Look closely, you'll see
the soft wrinkles of his trunk,
his lower stems have stopped growing.
                There's a problem somewhere –
                the roots will not hold water.
                He sloughs off his dying parts,
                drops cracked leaves and keeps climbing.
Both plants need care, are easy to care for.
He brings good luck, she fertility.
                I water them nightly, sing spiderettes to sleep
                in freshly made beds, while his coin
                fingers search
                her stem with the impatience of a newlywed.

From the Mouths of Babes

Yesterday I lost my temper.
Today I have a new temper.

Are we in love Mummy?
Yes, we are darling.

Where are you hiding?
Not in here!

You're taller than Granny,
one day I'll be taller than you.

Let's agree to disagree.
No, let's not.

Don't die until you've taught us to cook –
what would we eat?

It ends here

      he wears Cuban heels   Brut Paco Rabanne
her parents fear pregnancy   a door slams

     I invite him in
head against the wall   belt on the floor

keys daggered between my fingers   staccato breathing
                                          through the park
therapist's card folded twice
in my pocket   stood on a doorstep

     a flood of words   exhale
          it ends here

in the dappled light   my daughters dancing

Sister Sister

They remove each other's skin
and dive in,

breathe with one lung
set the other three free,

weave their long hair, strands of dark
strands of fair, to a soft rug

and lie together, float
warming water, hold hands

whisper plans only they know, fuse fingers and toes
into fleshy new clothes

move as one creature
in a web of their own.

Grandmothergram

adjective:
magnificent, impressive
noun:
slang for a thousand pounds / dollars
e.g. the childcare would've cost a grand

noun:
the female parent
of a child
verb:
to raise a child

Grand

Mother

definition:
the mother
of one's parent

Grandmother

informal:
granny / grandma
/ gran

idiom:
you can't teach a
grandmother to suck eggs

example:
sit down,
grandmother, and rest

meaning:
don't attempt to advise a
more experienced person

meaning:
stay alive a little longer,
please

Maman
After Louise Bourgeois

> We make, unmake, remake
> > to the sign of infinity,
>
> weave softness
> > to resilience,
>
> our silken net
> > studded with pearls of dew.
>
> A gossamer home, lit up
> > in the warm cradle
>
> of morning –
> > then they break through
>
> the web, and stride on,
> > brushing our sticky thread
>
> from their shoulders.

Night Birds

Walking in the garden, pulling bluebells
through arthritic fingers,

you tell me about the dusk chorus, how some
birds sing their loudest as the sun beds down.

We can hear them getting ready,
drawing air through their bills

down into lungs the size
of spider heads, air sacs

the bellows that inflate, deflate,
as tympanums vibrate.

One solitary note comes, then another,
bound to meet in flight.

Bird words collide like
blind arms embracing.

This is what we ageing creatures do:
drive our voices into the world

ink the sky with sound,
as night moves over the bluebells

searching for its place to be born.

Acknowledgements

Thanks are due to the following publications in which some of these poems, or earlier versions of them, first appeared: Atrium, Why Mums Are Amazing, The Mum Poet Guide to Self Care, Juno Magazine, The Hermeneutic Circular.

'Happiness' was shortlisted for the Exeter Poetry Prize 1999 and selected by Jo Shapcott to be published in the anthology of prize winners.

"Night Birds" was published in the anthology "Elements: Natural and the Supernatural" by Fawn Press 2021.

With many thanks to Rachel Long, Claire Walker, Rebecca Goss, Rebecca Tantony and Hollie McNish for their advice on individual poems.

I'm particularly grateful to Liz Berry and Dr Gemma Robinson for their invaluable feedback on the manuscript as a whole.

A massive thank you to Katharine Perry and Emma Dakeyne of amato & muldown for believing in my work, and to everyone at the Mum Poem Press and the Mum Poet Club for being so welcoming and supportive.

Thanks to Emma Dakeyne for creating the cover image for this book, and to Nomi Mcleod for drawing the beautiful inside illustrations.

Thanks to my father, for singing Edith Sitwell's Façade to me as a lullaby, and to our friend Fergus Chadwick for showing me the playful magic of poetry when I was a child. Thanks to the late George Whitman of Shakespeare & Co bookstore in Paris, and to my English teacher Richard Bush, both of whom encouraged me to write as a young adult.

I am grateful to my family and friends for their love and support.

Special thanks to my darling partner James, a wonderful spider father, and my first and best reader.

Advance Praise for *I am a Spider Mother*

This is a beautiful, tender book about raising twins and the webs we weave through the generations. In vivid poems, spun from the finest thread, the most intimate details of mothering are twined with the most profound. These are poems to connect us, as mothers and daughters; poems to treasure and share.

Liz Berry, author of *The Republic of Motherhood* and *Black Country*.

Flora Cruft's remarkable debut *I am a Spider Mother* is a poignant homage to motherhood and a monument to love that will stay with you long after you've finished reading. Emotionally resonant, written with precise, musical language, these luminous poems respond to memory, grief, hope, wonder, and beauty. They weave a magical 'silken net / studded with pearls of dew. / A gossamer home, lit up / in the warm cradle / of morning'.

Hélène Cardona, author of *Life in Suspension* and *Dreaming My Animal Selves*.

Not enough written about mothering twins! I loved it!

Hollie McNish, author of *Slug* and *Nobody Told Me*, about the poem *It's 4am* in *I am a Spider Mother*.

Lively, elegant and achingly beautiful poetry about motherhood and childhood. This collection is so unapologetically itself that it feels like reading someone's secrets. Comfortingly familiar ones. I found myself thinking "Yes, that's exactly it!"

Karen McMillan, author of *Mother Truths* and *Life Lessons*.

Flora Cruft's debut is an inventive and playfully experimental examination of the mother-daughter bond. Drawing on personal experience, Cruft leads us through tender inspections of the 'mellow honey' of childhood, and the 'sweet venom' of motherhood, sharing the ways in which different generations of women may hold and love each other.

Claire Walker, author of *Myth/Woman* and *Collision*.

A gentle yet poignant reflection on motherhood told from a variety of perspectives. The poems in this collection left me breathless at times in their ability to span generations, to reveal something personal and universal and offer it back with compassion and care. There is so much space for quiet and powerful reflection in these words, so much potential for learning and receiving the wisdom of loss and gain in turn.

Rebecca Tantony, author of *Singing My Mother's Song* and *All the Journeys I Never Took.*

I want poetry to drop me into a new feeling – good or bad – and I want it to make me feel my life, more. This wonderful book does that.

Clover Stroud, author of *My Wild And Sleepless Nights* and *The Wild Other.*

This is a collection that draws you in and sends you spinning beautifully between generations. Each poem stands alone as a finely wrought love song to motherhood. But it's the way the poems interconnect – rippling back and forth and gently breathing new layers of meaning into each other – that feels nothing short of magical. I loved this book, and can already tell I will come back to these poems again and again.

Jen Feroze, author of *The Colour of Hope.*

Bloody great poems, spider mother!

Laura Dockrill, author of *What Have I Done?* and *Echoes*.

A poignant, whimsical journey through maturation, motherhood and being mothered, *I am a Spider Mother* is a joy to read. Lyrical poems beautifully capture the tender, amazing moments of raising twins, as well as the challenges. As a fellow twin mum I found it evoked for me both the beauty and panic of having two babies. The intergenerational angle will ensure this book is treasured across the age range, and the creative layout adds to the pleasure of reading these moving, intimate poems.

Cath Counihan, psychotherapist and twin mum, @psychotherapy_mum

These thoughtful, incisive, beautiful poems spin vivid and affecting stories of mothers and daughters.

Ana Sampson, author of *Wonder: The Natural History Museum Poetry Book* and *Night Feeds and Morning Songs*.

I am a Spider Mother is such a spirited and heartfelt collection. A sustaining sense of connection weaves through each poem, from generation to generation, and to Mother Earth too. As tender as it is visceral, Cruft perfectly captures just how extraordinary motherhood really is.

Emlyia Hall, author of *The Thousand Lights Hotel* and *The Book of Summers*, and Founder of Mothership Writers.

This is a life-affirming volume, full of humour and wisdom. Every vivid poem left me with the sense of a scene, of a short story, above all of people in relationship. All is spoken with precision and clarity: 'Yesterday I lost my temper / Today I have a new temper.' Here is both celebration of life and affirmation of the struggle of mothering.

Perhaps most importantly the poet does her work of opening new pathways for our thinking. She goes before us to imagine phenomena and voice it so craftily that our thoughts are transplanted into new channels; as in the closing stanza from the book, where we are invited to stand in the garden at dusk and empathise with the night as it 'moves over the bluebells / searching for its place to be born.'

Anne Power, author of *Contented Couples*.